Phoni[...]

Reading Pr[...]

Let's See Grandma!

by Donna Taylor

Illustrated by Angel Rodriquez

Based on the books by Norman Bridwell

SCHOLASTIC INC.
New York Toronto London Auckland Sydney
Mexico City New Delhi Hong Kong Buenos Aires

"Clifford, we have to go to Grandma's. We will be back very soon," says Emily Elizabeth. "We will bring back a treat."

Her mother shuts the trunk.

And soon they drive away.

Clifford wants to see Grandma, too.

He will try to catch up to Emily Elizabeth and her mother.

He trots to the ferry.

Clifford misses the ferry.
He will try to take
a plane.

Clifford trots
to the airport.

"Sorry. No dogs!"
says the pilot.

Clifford trots to the dock.

"Sorry, Clifford,"
says Charley.
"You will sink the boat!"

"Hi, Clifford,"
says T-Bone.

"Why do you look
so grumpy?"

"Emily Elizabeth went
to Grandma's," Clifford
tells him.

"She will be back soon,"
says T-Bone. "You can
trust her."

Clifford trots home.

He drops down in the grass and feels sad.

But soon Emily Elizabeth and her mother come home.

Clifford sees that they did bring him a treat.

It is a great treat!

Grandma!